D0105139

To:

_____


From:

_____

# T.DAD Time

## MAX LUCADO

THOMAS NELSON
*Since 1798*

NASHVILLE   DALLAS   MEXICO CITY   RIO DE JANEIRO

Published in Nashville, Tennessee, by Thomas Nelson. Thomas Nelson is a registered trademark of HarperCollins Christian Publishing, Inc.

Cover design by Thinkpen Design.

Stock images p#/artist © Shutterstock: 6/Dubova, 24/Andrey Shchekalev, 40/Deklofenak, 56/Creativa, 82/BlueOrange Studio, 91/Maryna Pleshkun, 110/altanaka, 130/BlueOrange Studio, 142/altanaka, 156/Ganna Vasylenko

Thomas Nelson titles may be purchased in bulk for educational, business, fund-raising, or sales promotional use. For information, please e-mail SpecialMarkets@ThomasNelson.com.

ISBN: 978-0-52911-166-1

*Printed in the United States of America*

19 20 21 LSC 10 9 8 7 6 5

*For Jenna, Andrea, and Sara.*
*You'll never request too much,*
*call too late, or be too old.*
*I'm always your daddy.*

As a father has compassion on his
   children,
so the Lord has compassion on
   those who fear him.

                   Psalm 103:13

My daughters are too old for this now, but when they were young—crib-size and diaper-laden—I would come home, shout their names, and watch them run to me with extended arms and squealing voices. For the next few moments we would speak the language of love. We'd roll on the floor, gobble bellies, and tickle tummies and laugh and play.

We delighted in each other's presence. They made no requests of me, with the exception of "Let's play, Daddy." And I made no demands of them, except, "Don't hit Daddy with the hammer."

My kids let me love them.

—*Just Like Jesus*

Our kids were God's kids first. . . .
We tend to forget this fact, regarding our children as "our" children, as though we have the final say in their health and welfare. We don't. All people are God's people, including the small people who sit at our tables. Wise are the parents who regularly give their children back to God.

*—Fearless*

A father is the
one in your life
who provides
and protects.
That is exactly
what God
has done.

*—He Still Moves Stones*

# CONTENTMENT, MY DAUGHTER, AND ME

I remember a funny thing that happened on the way to the rat race that made me slip into neutral. Just as I got my sleeves rolled up, just as the old engine was starting to purr, just as I was getting up a good head of steam, my infant daughter, Jenna, needed to be held. She had a stomachache. Mom was in the bath so it fell to Daddy to pick her up.

She was three weeks old. At first I started trying to do things with one hand and hold her with the other. You're smiling. You've tried that too? Just when I realized that was impossible, I also realized that it was not at all what I was wanting to do.

I sat down and held her tight little tummy against my chest. She began to relax. A big sigh escaped her lungs. Her whimpers became gurgles. She slid down my chest until her little ear was right on top of my heart. That's when her arms went limp and she fell asleep. . . .

Good-bye, schedule. See you later, routine. Come back tomorrow, deadlines . . . hello, Contentment, come on in.

There we sat, Contentment, my daughter, and I. Pen in hand, note pad on Jenna's back. She'll never remember this moment and I'll never forget it.

—*No Wonder They Call Him the Savior*

We never outgrow our need for a father's love. We were wired to receive it.

—*Grace*

MAX LUCADO

*Children are a heritage from the L<small>ORD</small>,*
  *offspring a reward from him.*
*Like arrows in the hands of a warrior*
  *are children born in one's youth.*
*Blessed is the man*
  *whose quiver is full of them.*
                    P<small>SALM</small> 127:3–5

While parenting has its
problems and pitfalls, is there
any greater privilege?

—Max

# DESPERATE DADS
# GO TO JESUS

Jairus is the leader of the synagogue. That may not mean much to you and me, but in the days of Christ, the leader of the synagogue was the most important man in the community. The synagogue was the center of religion, education, leadership, and social activity. The leader of the synagogue was the senior religious leader, the highest-ranking professor, the mayor, and the best-known citizen all rolled into one.

Jairus has it all. Job security. A guaranteed welcome at the coffee shop. A pension plan. Golf every Thursday and an annual all-expenses-paid trip to the national convention.

Who could ask for more? Yet Jairus does. He *has* to ask for more. In fact, he would trade the whole package of perks and privileges for just one assurance—that his daughter will live.

The Jairus we see in this story is not the clear-sighted, black-frocked, nicely groomed civic leader. He is instead a blind man begging for a gift. He fell at Jesus' feet, saying again and again, "My little daughter is dying. Please come and put your hands on her so that she will be healed and live" (Mark 5:23).

He doesn't barter with Jesus. ("You do me a favor, and I'll see you are taken care of for life.") He doesn't negotiate with Jesus. ("The guys in Jerusalem are getting pretty testy about your antics. Tell you what, you handle this problem of mine, and I'll make a few calls. . . .") He doesn't make excuses. ("Normally, I'm not this desperate, Jesus, but I've got a small problem.")

He just pleads.

There are times in your life when everything you have to offer is nothing compared to what you are asking to receive. Jairus is at such a point. What could a man offer in exchange for his child's life? So there are no games. No haggling. No masquerades. The situation is starkly simple: Jairus is blind to the future and Jesus knows the future. So Jairus asks for help.

And Jesus, who loves the honest heart, goes to give it.

And God, who knows what it is like to lose a child, empowers his son.

*—He Still Moves Stones*

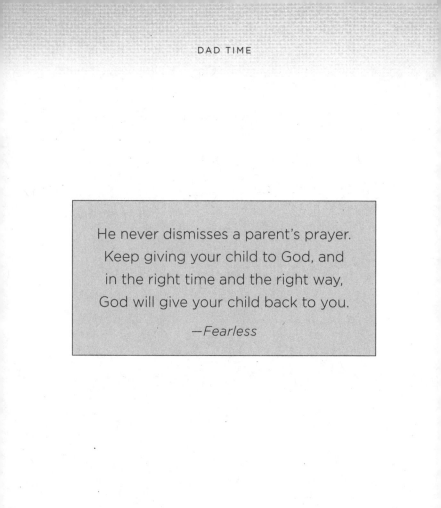

He never dismisses a parent's prayer.
Keep giving your child to God, and
in the right time and the right way,
God will give your child back to you.

—*Fearless*

Each year God gives millions of parents a gift, a brand-new baby. . . . Dads face a decision. Make our children in our images? Or release our children to follow their God-given identities?

Like no one else, parents can unlock the door to a child's uncommonness. As dads, we accelerate or stifle, release or repress our children's giftedness. They will spend much of life benefiting or recovering from our influence.

—*Cure for the Common Life*

Children
are like wet
cement. What
is modeled
for them
imprints their
character.

—Max

# IT'S NOT THE FRILLS;
# IT'S THE FATHER

One of my favorite childhood memories is greeting my father as he came home from work.

My mother, who worked an evening shift at the hospital, would leave the house around three in the afternoon. Dad would arrive home at three thirty. My brother and I were left alone for that half hour with strict instructions not to leave the house until Dad arrived.

We would take our positions on the couch and watch cartoons, always keeping one ear alert to the driveway. Even the best "Daffy Duck" would be abandoned when we heard his car.

I can remember running out to meet Dad and getting swept up in his big (often sweaty) arms. As he carried me toward the house, he'd put his big-brimmed straw hat on my head, and for a moment I'd be a cowboy. We'd sit on the porch as he removed his oily work boots (never allowed in the house). As he took them off I'd pull them on, and for a moment I'd be a wrangler. Then we'd go indoors and open his lunch pail. Any left-over snacks, which he always seemed to have, were for my brother and me to split.

It was great. Boots, hats, and snacks. What more could a five-year-old want?

But suppose, for a minute, that is all I got. Suppose my dad, rather than coming home, just sent some things home. Boots for me to play in. A hat for me to wear. Snacks for me to eat. . . .

No deal. That wouldn't work. Even a five-year-old knows it's the person, not the presents, that makes a reunion special. It's not the frills; it's the father.

—*When God Whispers Your Name*

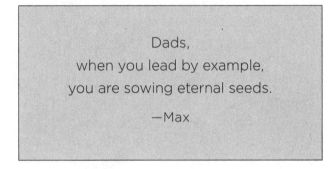

Dads,
when you lead by example,
you are sowing eternal seeds.

—Max

*Whoever fears the L*ORD *has a secure*
*   fortress,*
*      and for their children it will be a*
*   refuge.*

PROVERBS 14:26

At that moment
I realized
something.
I could look
around and
find fear, or I
could look at my
father and find
faith. I chose my
father's face.

*—It's Not about Me*

# THE FULL FORCE OF FATHERHOOD

No one told me that newborns make nighttime noises. All night long. They gurgle; they pant. They whimper; they whine. They smack their lips and sigh. They keep Daddy awake. At least Jenna kept me awake. I wanted Denalyn to sleep. Thanks to a medication mix-up, her post-C-section rest was scant. So for our first night home with our first child, I volunteered to serve as first responder. We wrapped our eight pounds and four ounces of beauty in a soft pink blanket, placed her in the bassinet, and set it next to my side of the bed. Denalyn fell quickly into a sound slumber. Jenna followed her mom's example. And Dad? This dad didn't know what to make of the baby noises.

When Jenna's breathing slowed, I leaned my ear onto her mouth to see if she was alive. When her breathing hurried, I looked up "infant hyperventilation" in the family medical encyclopedia. When she burbled and panted, so did I. After a couple of hours I realized, *I have no clue how to behave!* I lifted Jenna out of her bed, carried her into the living room of our apartment, and sat in a rocker. That's when a tsunami of sobriety washed over me.

"We're in charge of a human being."

I don't care how tough you are. You may be a Navy SEAL who specializes in high-altitude skydiving behind enemy lines. You might spend each day making million-dollar, split-second stock market decisions. Doesn't matter.

> *Every parent melts the moment he or she feels the full force of parenthood.*

I did.

*How did I get myself into this?* I retraced my steps. First came love, then came marriage, then the *discussions* of a baby carriage. Of course I was open to the idea. Especially when I considered my role in launching the effort. Somehow during the nine-month expansion project, the reality of fatherhood didn't dawn on me. But moms have an advantage: thirty-six weeks of reminders elbowing around inside them. Our kick in the gut comes later. But it does come. And for me it came years ago in the midnight quiet of an apartment living room in downtown Rio de Janeiro, Brazil, as I held a human being in my arms.

—*Fearless*

When I think about someone wiping away my tears, I think about Dad. His hands were callused and tough, his fingers short and stubby. And when my father wiped away a tear, he seemed to wipe it away forever. There was something in his touch that took away more than the drop of hurt from my cheek. It also took away my fear.

—*The Applause of Heaven*

No one can teach your child like you can. No nanny, Bible school teacher, aunt, or uncle has your authority. What a phenomenal privilege is yours.

—Max

# NO PRICE IS TOO HIGH

When our oldest daughter, Jenna, was two, I lost her in a department store. One minute she was at my side and the next she was gone. I panicked. All of a sudden only one thing mattered—I had to find my daughter. Shopping was forgotten. The list of things I came to get was unimportant. I yelled her name. What people thought didn't matter. For a few minutes, every ounce of energy had one goal—to find my lost child. (I did, by the way. She was hiding behind some jackets!)

No price is too high for a parent to pay to redeem his child. No energy is too great. No effort too demanding. A parent will go to any length to find his or her own.

So will God.

—*And the Angels Were Silent*

*Listen to your father, who gave you life.*

PROVERBS 23:22

Adopted children are chosen children. That's not the case with biological children. When the doctor handed Max Lucado to Jack Lucado, my dad had no exit option. No loophole. No choice. He couldn't give me back to the doctor and ask for a better-looking or smarter son. The hospital made him take me home.

But if you were adopted, your parents chose you. Surprise pregnancies happen. But surprise adoptions? Never heard of one. Your parents could have picked a different gender, color, or ancestry. But they selected you.

They wanted you in their family.

—*Grace*

# TIME IN A FATHER'S WORKSHOP

The highlight of my Cub Scout career was the Soap Box Derby. The competition was simple: construct a motorless go-cart and enter it in a downhill race. Some of the creations were fancy, complete with steering wheel and painted casing. Others were nothing more than a seat on a wooden chassis with four wheels and a rope for steering. My plan was to construct a genuine red roadster like the one in the Scout manual. Armed with a saw and hammer, a stack of lumber, and high ambition, I set out to be the Henry Ford of Troop 169.

I don't know how long my dad watched me before he interrupted my work. Probably not long, since my efforts weren't a pretty sight. The saw kept jamming and the wood kept buckling. The nails tended to bend and the panels didn't fit. At some point Dad mercifully intervened, tapped me on the shoulder, and told me to follow him into his workshop.

The small white frame house on the back of our lot was my dad's domain. I'd never really paid attention to what he did in there. All I knew was what I heard: buzzing saws, pounding hammers, and the whistle of a happy worker. I kept my bike in there, but I never noticed the tools. But then again, I'd never tried to build anything before. Over the next couple of hours that day, he introduced me to the magical world of sawhorses, squares, tape measures, and drills. He showed me how to draw a plan and measure the wood. He explained why it was wiser to hammer first and paint later. I was amazed. What was impossible for me was simple for him. Within an afternoon, we had constructed a pretty decent vehicle. And though I didn't leave the race with a trophy, I did leave with a greater admiration for my father. Why? Because I'd spent some time in his workshop.

—*The Great House of God*

You are loved by
your Maker not
because you try
to please him
and succeed, or
fail to please him
and apologize,
but because
he wants to be
your Father.

—*Grace*

Train up a child in the way he should go [and in keeping with his individual gift or bent], and when he is old he will not depart from it" (Proverbs 22:6 AMP).

Your baby has bents. Your toddler has tendencies. Your teen is set on a God-given trajectory. Discern it. Affirm it. Ask yourself, your spouse, and your friends: What is unique about this child? What does he excel in and where does he struggle? Observe strengths and weaknesses. Don't assume he or she is just like you. And don't assume your child is like another. Your kids are different. Discover and delight in that difference.

—Max

# A CALL FROM DAD MADE THE DIFFERENCE

Other events of my sixth-grade year blur into fog. I don't remember my grades or family holiday plans. I can't tell you the name of the brown-haired girl I liked or the principal of the school. But that spring evening in 1967? Crystal clear.

I'm seated in my parents' bedroom. Dinner conversation floats down the hallway. We have guests, but I asked to leave the table. Mom has made pie, but I passed on dessert. Not sociable. No appetite. Who has time for chitchat or pastry at such a time?

I need to focus on the phone.

I'd expected the call before the meal. It hadn't come. I'd listened for the ring during the meal. It hadn't rung. Now I'm staring at the phone like a dog at a bone, hoping a Little League coach will tell me I've made his baseball team.

I'm sitting on my bed, my glove at my side. I can hear my buddies playing out in the street. I don't care. All that matters is the phone. I want it to ring.

The guests leave. I help clean the dishes and finish my homework. Dad pats me on the back. Mom says kind words. Bedtime draws near. And the phone never rings. It sits in silence. Painful silence.

In the great scheme of things, not making a baseball team matters little. But twelve-year-olds can't see the great scheme of things, and it was a big deal, and all I could think about was what I would say when school-mates asked which team had picked me. . . .

Long after my hopes were gone and my glove was hung, the doorbell rang. It was the coach. He made it sound as if I were a top choice and he thought an assistant had phoned me. Only later did I learn the truth. I was the last pick. And, save a call from my dad, I might have been left off the team.

But Dad called, the coach came, and I was glad to play.

—*Facing Your Giants*

*Direct your children onto the right path,
and when they are older, they will
not leave it.*

PROVERBS 22:6 NLT

Straight teeth, straight As, straight posture cannot hold a candle compared to placing a child on the straight spiritual path. The highest privilege and purpose of a parent is to lead the child in the way of Christ. The towering questions for Christian parents are these: Do my kids know Christ? Have they tasted his grace and found comfort at his cross? Do they know their death is defeated and their hearts are empowered?

Parents, assignment number one is discipleship: help your child walk in the way of the Master.

—Max

# LOVING THE CHILD WHO DROPS THE BALL

Dropping a fly ball may not be a big deal to most people, but if you are thirteen years old and have aspirations of the big leagues, it is a big deal. Not only was it my second error of the game, it allowed the winning run to score.

I didn't even go back to the dugout. I turned around in the middle of left field and climbed over the fence. I was halfway home when my dad found me. He didn't say a word. Just pulled over to the side of the road, leaned across the seat, and opened the passenger door. We didn't speak. We didn't need to. We both knew the world had come to an end. When we got home, I went straight to my room, and he went straight to the kitchen. Presently he appeared in front of me with cookies and milk. He took a seat on the bed, and we broke bread together. Somewhere in the dunking of the cookies I began to realize that life and my father's love would go on. In the economy of male adolescence, if you love the guy who drops the ball, then you really love him. My skill as a baseball player didn't improve, but my confidence in Dad's love did. Dad never said a word. But he did show up. He did listen up. To bring out the best in others, do the same.

—*A Love Worth Giving*

Moments of comfort come from a parent. As a father, I can tell you they are the sweetest moments in my day.

—*The Applause of Heaven*

It is right to call God Holy; we speak truth when we call him King. But if you want to touch his heart, use the name he loves to hear. Call him *Father*.

—*The Great House of God*

# GOD IS YOUR CHILD'S FATHER TOO

God himself is a father. What parental emotion has he not felt? Are you separated from your child? So was God. Is someone mistreating your child? They mocked and bullied his. Is someone taking advantage of your child? The Son of God was set up by false testimony and betrayed by a greedy follower. Are you forced to watch while your child suffers? God watched his Son on the cross.

In addition, we are God's children, suffering in a world of sin that wreaks havoc on our bodies, twists our minds, and severs our relationships. Does God shrug his shoulders and say, "Oh well, that's life"? Of course not. Why would he go to all the trouble of introducing himself to the world with the title of Father? Curator, Manager, and Overseer are colder titles of indifference. God's role is not a job. It's a relationship. So God chose a relationship title you can identify with. Now you understand his heart when his children are in pain.

So whatever emotions you feel about your child, God feels about your child. Maybe more. I know that's hard to believe, but God has known your child longer than you have. He hurt for your child before he was born. You're not alone. Your Father weeps right by your side.

God is your child's Father too. Just as you'll do everything to help your child during his pain, so will God.

*—Max on Life*

D on't you see that children are G<small>OD</small>'s best gift? the fruit of the womb his generous legacy?" (Psalm 127:3 M<small>SG</small>). Before they were ours, they were his. Even as they are ours, they are still his.

—*Max on Life*

Imagine the joy you will feel when you stand before Christ, flanked by your wife and children . . . when your child says, "Thanks, Dad, for telling me about Christ."

—Max

# STUDY YOUR KIDS

Crankcase oil coursed my dad's veins. He repaired oil-field engines for a living and rebuilt car engines for fun. He worked in grease and bolts like sculptors work in clay; they were his media of choice. Dad loved machines.

But God gave him a mechanical moron, a son who couldn't differentiate between a differential and a brake disc. My dad tried to teach me. I tried to learn. Honestly, I did. But more than once I actually dozed off under the car on which we were working. Machines anesthetized me. But books fascinated me. I biked to the library a thousand times. What does a mechanic do with a son who loves books?

He gives him a library card. Buys him a few volumes for Christmas. Places a lamp by his bed so he can read at night. Pays tuition so his son can study college literature in high school. My dad did that. You know what he didn't do? Never once did he say, "Why can't you be a mechanic like your dad and granddad?" Maybe he understood my bent. Or maybe he didn't want me to die of hunger. . . .

Study your kids while you can. The greatest gift you can give your children is not your riches, but revealing to them their own.

—*Cure for the Common Life*

Before you change your job title, examine your perspective toward life. Success is not defined by position or pay scale but by this: doing the most what you do the best.

Dads, give that counsel to your kids. Tell them to do what they love to do so well that someone pays them to do it.

—*Cure for the Common Life*

*Tell to the generation to come the praises of*
    *the Lord,*
*And His strength and His wondrous*
    *works that He has done.*

PSALM 78:4 NASB

# "I'LL ALWAYS BE
THERE FOR YOU"

The 1989 Armenian earthquake needed only four minutes to flatten the nation and kill thirty thousand people. Moments after the deadly tremor ceased, a father raced to an elementary school to save his son. When he arrived, he saw that the building had been leveled. Looking at the mass of stones and rubble, he remembered a promise he had made to his child: "No matter what happens, I'll always be there for you." Driven by his own promise, he found the area closest to his son's room and began to pull back the rocks. Other parents arrived and began sobbing for their children. "It's too late," they told the man. "You know they are dead. You can't help." Even a police officer encouraged him to give up.

But the father refused. For eight hours, then sixteen, then thirty-two, thirty-six hours he dug. His hands were raw and his energy gone, but he refused to quit. Finally, after thirty-eight wrenching hours, he pulled back a boulder and heard his son's voice. He called his boy's name, "Arman! Arman!" And a voice answered him, "Dad, it's me!" Then the boy added these priceless words, "I told the other kids not to worry. I told them if you were alive, you'd save me, and when you saved me, they'd be saved, too. Because you promised, 'No matter what, I'll always be there for you.'"[1]

—*When Christ Comes*

I can't assure you that your family will
ever give you the blessing you seek,
but I know God will. Let God give
you what your family doesn't. If your
earthly father doesn't affirm you, then
let your heavenly Father take his place.

—*Max on Life*

Maybe, like Joseph, you're dad to a child who isn't your flesh and blood. Maybe you are a stepdad, an adoptive dad, a grandpa raising grandkids. If that is you, know this: God must think highly of you. He has called you to step into an empty spot and fill the role. He has called you to be Joseph in the life of a young child. May you do what Joseph did. May you so love that child that they'd think you were their father. That child may not have your eyes or nose or even your name. But they can have your love.

—Max

# DAD'S GIFT OF GRACE

My father had a simple rule about credit cards: own as few as possible and pay them off as soon as possible. His salary as a mechanic was sufficient but not abundant, and he hated the thought of paying interest. He made it a point to pay the balance in full at the end of the month. You can imagine my surprise when he put a credit card in my hand the day I left for college.

Standing in the driveway with a car packed and farewells said, he handed it to me. I looked at the name on the plastic; it wasn't mine, it was his. He had ordered an extra card for me. His only instructions to me were, "Be careful how you use it." . . .

Did I mention that I went several months without needing it? But when I needed it, I *really* needed it. You see, I wanted to visit a friend on another campus. Actually, the friend was a girl in another city, six hours away. On an impulse I skipped class one Friday morning and headed out. Not knowing whether my parents would approve, I didn't ask their permission. Because I left in a hurry, I forgot to take any money. I made the trip without their knowledge and with an empty wallet.

Everything went fine until I rear-ended a car on the return trip. Using a crowbar, I pried the fender off my front wheel so the car could limp to a gas station. I can still envision the outdoor phone where I stood in the autumn chill. My father, who assumed I was on campus, took my collect call and heard my tale. My story wasn't much to boast about. I'd made a trip without his knowledge, without any money, and wrecked his car.

"Well," he said after a long pause, "these things happen. That's why I gave you the card. I hope you learned a lesson."

Did I learn a lesson? I certainly did. I learned that my father's forgiveness predated my mistake. He had given me the card before my wreck in the event that I would have one. He had provided for my blunder before I blundered. Need I tell you that God has done the same? Please understand; Dad didn't want me to wreck the car. He didn't give me the card so that I would wreck the car. But he knew his son. And he knew his son would someday need grace.

—*In the Grip of Grace*

Jesus heeds the concern in the parent's heart. After all, our kids were his kids first.

*—Fearless*

The love of a parent for a child is a mighty force. Consider the couple with their new-born child. The infant offers his parents absolutely nothing. No money. No skill. No words of wisdom. If he had pockets, they would be empty. To see an infant lying in a bassinet is to see utter help-lessness. What is there to love?

Whatever it is, Mom and Dad find it. Just watch Dad's eyes as he cradles the child. And just try to harm or speak evil of the infant. If you do, you'll encounter a mighty strength, for the love of a parent is a mighty force.

—*He Chose the Nails*

# A DAD'S COMMITMENT

When I was seven years old, I ran away from home. I'd had enough of my father's rules and decided I could make it on my own, thank you very much. With my clothes in a paper bag, I stormed out the back gate and marched down the alley. Like the prodigal son, I decided I needed no father. Unlike the prodigal son, I didn't go far. I got to the end of the alley and remembered I was hungry, so I went back home.

Though the rebellion was brief, it was rebellion nonetheless. Had you stopped me on that prodigal path and asked me who my father was, I just might have said, "I don't need a father. I'm too big for the rules of my family. It's just me, myself, and my paper bag." I don't remember saying that to anyone, but I remember thinking it. And I also remember rather sheepishly stepping in the back door and taking my seat at the supper table across from the very father I had, only moments before, disowned.

Did Dad know of my insurrection? I suspect he did. Did he know of my denial? Fathers usually do. Was I still his son? Apparently so. (No one else was sitting in my place at the table.) Suppose, after speaking to me, you had gone to my father and asked, "Mr. Lucado, your son says he has no need of a father. Do you still consider him your son?" What do you think my dad would have said?

I don't have to guess at his answer. He called himself my father even when I didn't call myself his son. His commitment to me was greater than my commitment to him.

—*Max on Life*

In direct contrast to a culture that devalues children, God places them in a special place. "One day some parents brought their children to Jesus so he could touch them and bless them. But the disciples scolded the parents for bothering him. When Jesus saw what was happening, he was angry with his disciples. He said to them, 'Let the children come to me. Don't stop them! For the Kingdom of God belongs to those who are like these children. I tell you the truth, anyone who doesn't receive the Kingdom of God like a child will never enter it.' Then he took the children in his arms and placed his hands on their heads and blessed them" (Mark 10:13–16 NLT).

There was once a person in our world who brought Denalyn and me a lot of stress. She would call in the middle of the night. She was demanding and ruthless. She screamed at us in public. When she wanted something, she wanted it immediately, and she wanted it exclusively from us.

But we never asked her to leave us alone. We never told her to bug someone else. We never tried to get even.

After all, she was only a few months old.

It was easy for us to forgive our infant daughter's behavior because we knew she didn't know better.

—*Max on Life*

# A CLOSE CALL

I remember the day as a sunny, summer Brazilian one. Denalyn and I were spending the afternoon with our friends Paul and Debbie. Their house was a welcome respite. We lived close to downtown Rio de Janeiro in a high-rise apartment. Paul and Debbie lived an hour away from the city center in a nice house where the air was cooler, the streets were cleaner, and life was calmer. Besides, they had a swimming pool.

Our two-year-old daughter, Jenna, loved to play with their kids. And that is exactly what she was doing when she fell. We didn't intend to leave the children unattended. We had stepped into the house for just a moment to fill our plates. We were chatting and chewing when Paul and Debbie's four-year-old walked into the room and casually told her mom, "Jenna fell in the pool." We exploded out the door. Jenna was flopping in the water, wearing neither floaties nor a life jacket. Paul reached her first. He jumped in and lifted her up to Denalyn. Jenna coughed and cried for a minute, and just like that she was fine. Tragedy averted. Daughter safe.

Imagine our gratitude. We immediately circled up the kids, offered a prayer, and sang a song of thanks. For the remainder of the day, our feet didn't touch the ground, and Jenna didn't leave our arms. Even driving home, I was thanking God. In the rearview mirror I could see Jenna sound asleep in her car seat, and I offered yet another prayer: *God, you are so good.* Then a question surfaced in my thoughts. From God? Or from the part of me that struggles to make sense out of God? I can't say. But what the voice asked, I still remember: *If Jenna hadn't survived, would God still be good?*

I had spent the better part of the afternoon broadcasting God's goodness. Yet had we lost Jenna, would I have reached a different verdict? Is God good only when the outcome is?

The definitive answer comes in the person of Jesus Christ. Do you want to know heaven's clearest answer to the question of suffering? Just look at the cross. He exacts nothing from us that he did not experience himself.

Why? Because he is good.

—*You'll Get Through This*

Christ is passionately protective of children. "If you cause one of these little ones who trusts in me to fall into sin, it would be better for you to have a large millstone tied around your neck and be drowned in the depths of the sea" (Matthew 18:6 NLT).

God loves kids with a protective passion. Do the same. At the risk of stating the obvious, decide your kids are worth it.

They are worth the dirty diapers, shortened nights, tight budgets, and carpools. They are your mission in life! In short order, they will be gone. Lead them in the way of the Master while you can! Yes, it's costly, but it's easier to train children than to repair adults.

—Max

# WHAT PLEASES A FATHER

When our daughters were young, Denalyn went away for a couple of days and left me alone with the girls. Though the time was not without the typical children's quarrels and occasional misbehavior, it went fine.

"How were the girls?" Denalyn asked when she got home.

"Good. No problem at all."

Jenna overheard my response. "We weren't good, Daddy," she objected. "We fought once; we didn't do what you said once. We weren't good. How can you say we were good?"

Jenna and I had different perceptions of what pleases a father. She thought it depended on what she did. It didn't. We think the same about God. We think his love rises and falls with our performance. It doesn't. I didn't love Jenna for what she did. I loved her—and love her still—for whose she is. She is mine.

God loves you for the same reason. He loves you for whose you are; you are his child. (Romans 8:16)

—*And the Angels Were Silent*

Fathers, do not make your children angry, but raise them with the training and teaching of the Lord.

*Ephesians 6:4* NCV

# A SONG FOR DAD

I remember many years ago when I was in Atlanta, Georgia, at a conference. I called home and talked to Denalyn and the girls. Jenna was about five at the time and said she had a special treat for me. She took the phone over to the piano and began to play an original composition.

From a musical standpoint, everything was wrong with the song. She pounded more than she played. There was more random than rhythm in the piece. The lyrics didn't rhyme. The syntax was sinful. Technically the song was a failure.

But to me, the song was a masterpiece. Why? Because she wrote it for me.

> *You are a great daddy.*
> *I miss you very much.*
> *When you're away I'm very sad and I cry.*
> *Please come home very soon.*

What dad wouldn't like that?

—*And the Angels Were Silent*

71

Our kids live in a performance-based world.

- The better the test, the better the grade.
- The faster the run, the higher they place.
- The prettier they are, the more they are liked.
- The thinner they are, the more they are noticed.

Day in, day out, the world tells our kids: "you are only as good as your performance." What words do your children hear from you?

—Max

# SEEKING THE SACRED

When my daughters were young, I would write late at night. Not necessarily because I wanted to, but because sanity only came to our house after the ten o'clock news.

From the moment I got home in the afternoon to the minute I sat down at the computer some five hours later, the motion was nonstop. Within thirty seconds of my entering the door, both of my knees were attacked by two squealing girls. A fuzzy-headed infant was placed in my arms and a welcome-home kiss was planted on my lips.

"The cavalry is here," I announced.

"And none too soon," my wife, Denalyn, replied with a grateful smile.

The next few hours would bring a chorus of family noises: giggles, clanging dishes, rumbles on the floor, screams of agony over stumped toes, splashes in the bath, and thuds from toys tossed in the basket. The conversation was as continuous as it was predictable.

"Can I have more pie?"

"Jenna has my doll!"

"Can I hold the baby?"

"Honey, where is the pacifier?"

"Are there any clean gowns in the dryer?"

"Girls, it's time to go to bed."

"One more song?"

Then, eventually, the nightly hurricane passed, and the roar subsided. Mom looked at Dad. The day's damage was surveyed and cleaned up. Mom went to bed and Dad went into the playroom to write.

I would sit in the stillness accompanied by the tap of a computer keyboard, the aroma of coffee, and the rhythm of the dishwasher. What was a playroom thirty minutes ago was now a study. And what was a study now may—just may—become a sanctuary. For what happened in the next few minutes bordered on the holy.

The quietness would slow my pulse, the silence would open my ears, and something sacred would happen. The soft slap of sandaled feet would break the stillness, a pierced hand would extend a quiet invitation, and I would follow.

I wish I could say it happened every night; it didn't. Some nights he asked and I didn't listen. Other nights he asked and I just didn't go. But some nights I heard his poetic whisper, "Come to me, all you who are weary and burdened . . ." (Matthew 11:28) and I followed. I left behind the budgets, bills, and deadlines and walked the narrow trail up the mountain with him.

—*The Applause of Heaven*

Yes, your family history has some sad chapters. But your history doesn't have to be your future. The generational garbage can stop here and now. You don't have to give your kids what your ancestors gave you. . . .

"Let God transform you into a new person by changing the way you think" (Romans 12:2 NLT). Let him replace childish thinking with mature truth (1 Corinthians 13:11). You are not who they said you were. You are God's child. His creation. Destined for heaven. You are a part of his family. Let him set you on the path to reconciliation.

—*You'll Get Through This*

# "I WANT A *NEW* DADDY!"

Some time ago, I took my family to the bicycle store to purchase a bike for five-year-old Jenna. She picked out a shiny "Starlett" with a banana seat and training wheels. And Andrea, age three, decided she wanted one as well.

I explained to Andrea that she was too young. I told her she was still having trouble with a tricycle and was too small for a two-wheeler. No luck; she still wanted a bike. I explained to her that when she was bit older, she would get a bike too. I tried to tell her that a big bike would bring her more pain than pleasure, more scrapes than thrills. She turned her head and said nothing.

Finally I sighed and said this time her daddy knew best. Her response? She screamed it loud enough for everyone in the store to hear:

"Then I want a *new* daddy!" . . .

Andrea, with her three-year-old reasoning powers,

couldn't believe that a new bike would be anything less than ideal for her. From her vantage point, the one who could grant that bliss was "sitting on his hands." . . .

If you've heard the silence of God, you may learn that the problem is not as much in God's silence as it is in your ability to hear.

—*The Applause of Heaven*

God prewired your infant. He sculpted your toddler's strengths. He set your teen on a trajectory. God gave you an eighteen-year research project. Ask yourself, your spouse, and your friends: What sets this child apart? Childhood tendencies forecast adult abilities. Read them. Discern them. Affirm them. Cheerlead them.

—*Cure for the Common Life*

# SHE CALLED ME DADDY

When my daughter Sara was in the second grade, we took her desk hunting at a store that specializes in unpainted furniture. She was excited about owning her own desk. When she learned we weren't taking the desk home that day, she was upset. "But, Daddy, I wanted to take it home today."

Much to her credit, she didn't stomp her feet and demand her way. She did, however, set out on an urgent course to change her father's mind. Every time I turned a corner, she was waiting for me.

"Daddy, don't you think we could paint it ourselves?"

"Daddy, I just want to draw some pictures on my new desk."

"Daddy, please, let's take it home today."

After a bit she disappeared, only to return, arms open wide, bubbling with a discovery. "Guess what, Daddy. It'll fit in the back of the car!"

You and I know that a seven-year-old has no clue what will or won't fit in a vehicle, but the fact that she had measured the trunk with her arms softened my heart. The clincher, though, was the name she called me: Daddy.

The Lucado family took a desk home that day.

—*The Great House of God*

I was moved to respond because Sara called me "Daddy." Because she is my child, I heard her request. Because we are his children, God hears ours.

—*The Great House of God*

My child's feelings are hurt. I tell her she's special. My child is injured. I do whatever it takes to make her feel better.

My child is afraid. I won't go to sleep until she is secure.

I'm not a hero. I'm not a superstar. I'm not unusual. I'm a parent. When a child hurts, a parent does what comes naturally. He helps.

*—The Applause of Heaven*

# A LESSON ON GRACE

L emonade, 5¢"

The *e* is larger than the *L*. The *m* is uppercased; all the other letters are lowered. The last two letters, *de*, curve downward because the artist ran out of room on the poster board.

Norman Rockwell would have loved it.

Two girls sit on the sidewalk in little chairs behind a little table. The six-year-old is the cashier. She monitors a plastic bowl of change. The four-year-old is the waitress. She handles the ice. Pours the drinks. Stacks and restacks the paper cups.

Behind them, seated on the grass, is Dad. He leans against an oak tree and smiles as he witnesses his daughters' inauguration into capitalism.

Business has been steady. The Saturday-afternoon stream of patrons has nearly emptied the pitcher. The bottom of the cashier's bowl is covered with thirty-five cents of change. With the exception of a few spills, the service has been exceptional. No complaints. Many compliments.

Part of the success, though, has been due to the marketing strategy.

Our street doesn't get much traffic, so we did a little advertising. As my daughters painted the sign, I called several families in the neighborhood and invited them to the grand opening of our lemonade stand. So all of our clients, thus far, had been partial.

I was proud of myself. I leaned back against the tree. Closed my eyes. Turned up the radio I had brought. And listened to the baseball game.

Then I heard an unfamiliar voice.

"I'll have a cup of lemonade, please."

*I opened my eyes. It was a customer. A real customer.*

An unsolicited neighbor who had driven by, seen the sign, stopped, and ordered a drink.

*Uh-oh*, I thought. Our service was about to be tested.

Andrea, the four-year-old, grabbed a cup that had already been used.

"Get a clean cup," I whispered.

"Oh," she giggled, and got a clean cup.

She opened the ice bucket, looked in, and then looked back at me. "Daddy, we are out of ice."

The patron overheard her. "That's OK. I'll take it warm."

She picked up the pitcher and poured. Syrupy sugar oozed out of the pitcher. "Daddy, there's just a little bit."

Our customer spoke again. "That's fine. I don't want much."

"I hope you like it sweet," I said under my breath.

She handed the cup to the man, and he handed her a dollar. She gave it to Jenna.

Jenna turned to me. "Daddy, what do I do?" (We weren't used to such big bills.)

I stuck my hands in my pockets; they were empty.

"Uh, we don't have any . . ." I began.

"No problem," he said, smiling. "Just keep the change."

I smiled sheepishly. He thanked the girls. Told them they were doing a great job. Climbed back into his car. And drove off.

*Quite a transaction,* I thought. *We give him a warm, partially filled cup of lemonade syrup, and he gives us a compliment and a payment twenty times too much.*

I had set out to teach the girls about free enterprise. They ended up with a lesson on grace.

—*In the Eye of the Storm*

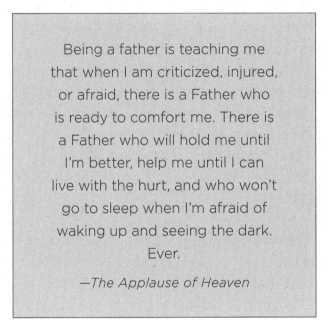

Being a father is teaching me
that when I am criticized, injured,
or afraid, there is a Father who
is ready to comfort me. There is
a Father who will hold me until
I'm better, help me until I can
live with the hurt, and who won't
go to sleep when I'm afraid of
waking up and seeing the dark.
Ever.

—*The Applause of Heaven*

You can't control what your kids hear from the world. But you can control what they hear from you.

When my oldest daughter, Jenna, was four years old, she came to me with a confession. "Daddy, I took a crayon and drew on the wall." (Kids amaze me with their honesty.)

I sat down and lifted her up into my lap and tried to be wise. "Is that a good thing to do?" I asked her.

"No."

"What does Daddy do when you write on the wall?"

"You spank me."

"What do you think Daddy should do this time?"

"Love."

Don't we all want that?

—*Six Hours One Friday*

# DADS KNOW THE WAY HOME

took my daughter Andrea on a walk some time ago. She was four and curious, so we went to explore our neighborhood. "Let's cover some new territory," I suggested. Off we went, striding confidently out of the safe harbor of our cul-de-sac and stepping into unknown regions.

Captain Kirk would have been proud.

The area was brand new to her. We walked down streets she'd never seen and petted dogs she'd never touched. Virgin territory. Wilderness wanderings. The yards were different. The kids looked older. The houses looked bigger.

I thought all the change might trouble her. I thought the new sights and sounds might generate anxiety.

"Are you okay?" I asked.

"Sure."

"Do you know where we are?"

"No."

"Do you know how to get home?"

"No."

"And you aren't worried?"

Without slowing her pace, she reached up and took my hand and said, "I don't have to know how to get home. You already do."

*—And the Angels Were Silent*

# CATCHING YOUR CHILD

I stand six steps from the bed's edge. My arms extended. Hands open. On the bed, Sara—all four years of her—crouches, poised like a playful kitten. She's going to jump. But she's not ready. I'm too close.

"Back more, Daddy." she stands and dares.

I dramatically comply, confessing admiration for her courage. After two giant steps I stop. "More?" I ask.

"Yes!" Sara squeals, hopping on the bed.

With each step she laughs and claps and motions for more. When I'm on the other side of the canyon, when I'm beyond the reach of mortal man, when I am but a tiny figure on the horizon, she stops me. "There, stop there."

"Are you sure?"

"I'm sure," she shouts. I extend my arms. Once again she crouches, then springs. Superman without a cape. Skydiver without a chute. Only her heart flies higher than her body. In that airborne instant her only hope is her father. If he proves weak, she'll fall. If he proves cruel, she'll crash. If he proves forgetful, she'll tumble to the hard floor.

But such fear she does not know, for her father she does. She trusts him. Four years under the same roof have convinced her he is reliable. He is not superhuman, but he is strong. He is not holy, but he is good. He's not brilliant, but he doesn't have to be to remember to catch his child when she jumps.

And so she flies.

And so she soars. . . .

The next time you wonder if you will survive the jump, think of Sara and me. If a flesh-and-boneheaded dad like me can catch his child, don't you think your eternal Father can catch you?

—*When God Whispers Your Name*

# A FATHER'S FINAL LETTER

There is nothing impressive about the stationery. No embossed letters. No watermark. No heavy stock paper. Just a sheet of legal-pad paper, the top of which is jagged from the tear.

There is nothing impressive about the handwriting. There used to be. As a child, I tried to imitate it. But you wouldn't want to imitate this penmanship; you'd be hard-pressed to decipher it. Angled lines. Irregular letters and inconsistent spacing.

But it was the best my father could do. Lou Gehrig's disease had so weakened his hands he could scarcely bring a fork to his mouth, much less write words on a page. Imagine writing with all your fingers wrapped around the pen, and you're close to understanding his challenge.

It was the final letter he wrote us. The ALS and cold weather had nearly killed him. Denalyn and I had rushed home from Brazil and spent a month eating hospital food and taking shifts at his bedside. He rebounded, however, so we returned to South America. A day or so after arriving, we received this letter.

*January 19, 1984*

> *Dear Max and Denalyn,*
>
> *We were glad you all made it home OK. Now settle down and get to work. We enjoyed your trip to no end. Even your spending the nights with me.*
>
> *MAX, YOU AND DENALYN ALWAYS STICK TOGETHER, WHATEVER HAPPENS.*
>
> *Well, there is no need of me scribbling. I think you know how much I love you both. You all just live good Christian lives and FEAR GOD.*
>
> *I hope to see you again on earth—if not, I will in heaven.*
>
> > *Lots of love,*
> > *Dad*

I've envisioned my father writing those words. Propped up in a hospital bed, pen in hand, pad on lap.

Thinking this would be his final message. Do you suppose he chose his words carefully? Of course he did.

Can you envision trying to do the same? Can you imagine your final message to those you love? Your last words with a child or spouse?

What would you say? How would you say it?

—*He Chose the Nails*

> *The righteous man walks in his integrity;*
> *His children are blessed after him.*
>
> PROVERBS 20:7 NKJV

I once asked my dad what he thought I should do as an adult. He was a mechanic. His dad was a mechanic. Three of his brothers worked on engines. You might expect him to urge me to do the same. But he'd seen me change the oil. He knew better. So he said, "Do what you love to do." Such words set a child free.

—Max

# WE ALL NEED A FATHER

When my daughter Jenna was twelve, she and I spent several days in the old city of Jerusalem. (I took each of my daughters to Jerusalem when they were twelve years old. Got the idea from Joseph.) One afternoon, as we were exiting the Jaffa gate, we found ourselves behind an orthodox Jewish family—a father and his three small girls. One of the daughters, perhaps four or five years of age, fell a few steps behind and couldn't see her father. *"Abba!"* she called to him. He stopped and looked. Only then did he realize he was separated from his daughter. *"Abba!"* she called again. He spotted her and immediately extended his hand. She took it and I took mental notes as they continued. I wanted to see the actions of an *abba*.

He held her hand tightly in his as they descended the ramp. When he stopped at a busy street, she stepped off the curb, so he pulled her back. When the signal changed, he led her and her sisters through the intersection. In the middle of the street, he reached down and swung her up into his arms and continued the journey.

Isn't that what we all need? An *abba* who will hear when we call? Who will take our hand when we're weak? Who will guide us through the hectic intersections of life? Don't we all need an *abba* who will swing us up in his arms and carry us home? We all need a father.

—*The Great House of God*

Parents, we can't protect children from every threat in life, but we can take them to the Source of life. We can entrust our kids to Christ.

—*Fearless*

# A GIFT FOR MY DAUGHTERS

I remember when the whirlwind of adolescence was making regular runs through our house, bringing with it more than our share of doubts, pimples, and peer pressure. I couldn't protect the girls from the winds, but I could give them an anchor to hold in the midst. On Valentine's Day, 1997, I wrote the following and had it framed for each daughter:

*I have a special gift for you. My gift is warmth at night and sunlit afternoons, chuckles and giggles and happy Saturdays.*

*But how do I give this gift? Is there a store which sells laughter? A catalog that offers kisses? No. Such a treasure can't be bought. But it can be given. And here is how I give it to you.*

*Your Valentine's Day gift is a promise: a promise that I will always love your mother. With God as my helper, I will never leave her. You'll never come home to find me gone. You'll never wake up and find that I have run away. You'll always have two parents. I will love your mother. I will honor your mother. I will cherish your mother. That is my promise. That is my gift.*

*Love, Dad*

*—A Love Worth Giving*

We parents have it especially tough. I remember when my daughters were at that age when they were starting to drive. It seemed like just days before I was teaching them to walk, and not putting them behind a steering wheel. It was a scary thought. I thought of making a special bumper sticker for Jenna's car that reads "How am I driving? 1-800-CALL-DAD."

—*He Chose the Nails*

# SUCCEED AT HOME FIRST

Quiet heroes dot the landscape of our society. They don't wear ribbons or kiss trophies; they wear spit-up and kiss boo-boos. They don't make the headlines, but they do sew the hemlines and check the outlines and stand on the sidelines. You won't find their names on the Nobel Prize short list, but you will find their names on the homeroom, carpool, and Bible teacher lists.

They are parents, both by blood and deed, name and calendar. Heroes. News programs don't call them. But that's okay. Because their kids do . . . They call them Mom. They call them Dad. And these moms and dads, more valuable than all the executives and lawmakers west of the Mississippi, quietly hold the world together.

Be numbered among them. Read books to your kids. Play ball while you can and they want you to. Make it your aim to watch every game they play, read every story they write, hear every recital in which they perform.

Children spell love with four letters: T-I-M-E. Not just quality time, but hang time, downtime, anytime, all the time. Your children are not your hobby; they are your calling. . . .

Cherish the children who share your name.

Succeed at home first.

—*Facing Your Giants*

Never miss
a chance
to read
a child
a story.

—*When God Whispers Your Name*

Discipline is an essential part of parenting. While God promotes it, he also calls for the mature application of it. Here are four rules for discipline:

1. *Be careful.* Be quick to interrupt misbehavior but slow to punish it. Place a child in time-out while you both cool down. Punishment is never a license for cruelty. If you are enjoying the administration of the discipline, you need to stop.

2. *Be consistent.* The punishment must fit the act. Seek to discern the cause of action. What motivated this behavior? It's one thing to slam a door out of disrespect. It's another to slam it because the ice cream truck is on the street. Forgetting to clean the room is one matter; stamping a foot and refusing to do it is another. Oversights are misdemeanors. Rebellion is a felony.

3. *Be clear.* Explain what the punishment is and what the offense was. Do not assume the

child understands. Do not punish a child for "being bad." The child may have done a bad thing, but that doesn't mean he is a bad child.

4. *Be compassionate.* One mistake does not a child make. One season of waywardness does not a child define. "[Love] keeps no record of wrongs" (1 Corinthians 13:5). But love does keep a list of things done well.

—Max

*The father of a righteous child has great joy;*
*a man who fathers a wise son rejoices in*
*him.*

PROVERBS 23:24

# A LIFE WELL LIVED

Years ago, on a trip to my hometown, I took some time to go see a tree. "A live oak tree," my dad had called it (with the accent on "live"). It was nothing more than a sapling, so thin I could wrap my hand around it and touch my middle finger to my thumb. The West Texas wind scattered the fall leaves and caused me to zip up my coat. There is nothing colder than a prairie wind, especially in a cemetery.

"A special tree," I said to myself, "with a special job." I looked around. The cemetery was lined with elms but no oaks. The ground was dotted with tombstones but no trees. Just this one. A special tree for a special man.

At first Daddy began noticing a steady weakening of his muscles. It began in his hands. He then felt it in his calves. Next his arms thinned a bit.

He mentioned his condition to my brother-in-law, who is a physician. My brother-in-law, alarmed, sent him to a specialist. The specialist conducted a lengthy battery of tests—blood, neurological, and muscular—and he reached his conclusion. Lou Gehrig's disease. A devastating crippler. No one knows the cause or the cure. The only sure thing about it is its cruelty and accuracy.

I remember looking down at the plot of ground that would someday entomb my father. Daddy always wanted to be buried under an oak tree so he bought this one. "Special order from the valley," he had boasted. "Had to get special permission from the city council to put it here." (That wasn't hard in this dusty oil field town where everybody knows everybody.)

The lump got tighter in my throat. A lesser man might have been angry. Another man might have given up. But Daddy didn't.

*He knew that his days were numbered*
*so he began to get his house in order.*

The tree was only one of the preparations he made. He improved the house for Mom by installing a sprinkler system and a garage door and by painting the trim.

He got the will updated. He verified the insurance and retirement policies. He bought some stock to go toward his grandchildren's education. He planned his funeral. He bought cemetery plots for himself and Mom. He prepared his kids through words of assurance and letters of love. And last of all, he bought the tree. A live oak tree. (Pronounced with an accent on "live.")

Final acts. Final hours. Final words.

They reflect a life well lived.

—*No Wonder They Call Him the Savior*

In the rough
and tumble of
bad weather, we
need an outside
force. We need
a guide that is
unaffected by
storms. Don't
listen to your
friends. Listen
to your Father.

*—Max on Life*

Envision a father helping his son learn to ride a bicycle. The father stays at the son's side. He pushes the bike and steadies it if the boy starts to tumble. The Spirit does the same for us; he stays our step and strengthens our stride. Unlike the earthly father who eventually releases his grip on the bike and allows his son to journey down the road on his own, the Holy Spirit never leaves. He is with us to the end of the age.

—*Max on Life*

# YOUR CHILDREN WANT
# YOU FOR WHO YOU ARE

There's only so much sand in the hourglass. Who gets it?

You know what I'm talking about, don't you? . . .

"The PTA needs a new treasurer. With your background and experience and talent and wisdom and love for kids and degree in accounting, YOU are the perfect one for the job!"

"There's going to be some shuffling in the ranks. With the retirement of the branch manager, *somebody* will move up. The company is looking for a bright, young salesman—someone like you—who is willing to demonstrate his dedication to the organization by taking on some extra projects . . . and working some late hours." . . .

It's a tug-of-war, and you are the rope.

On one side are the requests for your time and

energy. They call. They compliment. They are valid and good. Great opportunities to do great things. If they were evil, it'd be easy to say no. But they aren't, so it's easy to rationalize.

On the other side are the loved ones in your world. They don't write you letters. They don't ask you to consult your calendar. They don't offer to pay your expenses. They don't use terms like "appointment," "engagement," or "do lunch." They don't want you for what you can do for them; they want you for who you are.

—*In the Eye of the Storm*

The fifth commandment does not say, "Honor your God-fearing mother and father who have a Christian worldview." It says, "Honor your father and your mother" (Exodus 20:12). Period. There's no specification about their beliefs. So honor them by at least hearing what they have to say.

—*Max on Life*

# DON'T MAKE
# DAVID'S MISTAKE

David succeeded everywhere except at home. And if you don't succeed at home, do you succeed at all? David would have benefitted from the counsel of Paul the apostle: "Fathers, do not provoke your children to anger by the way you treat them" (Ephesians 6:4 NLT).

How do we explain David's disastrous home? How do we explain David's silence when it comes to his family? No psalms are written about his children. Surely out of all his wives, one was worthy of a sonnet or song? But he never talked about them.

Aside from the prayer he offered for Bathsheba's baby, Scripture gives no indication that he ever prayed for his family. He prayed about the Philistines, interceded for his warriors. He offered prayers for Jonathan, his friend, and for Saul, his archrival. But as far as his family is concerned, it's as if they never existed.

Was David too busy to notice them? Maybe. He had a city to settle and a kingdom to build.

Was he too important to care for them? "Let the wives raise the kids; I'll lead the nation."

Was he too guilty to shepherd them? After all, how could David, who had seduced Bathsheba and intoxicated and murdered Uriah, correct his sons when they raped and murdered?

Too busy. Too important. Too guilty. And now? Too late. A dozen exits too late. But it's not too late for you. Your home is your giant-size privilege, your towering priority. Do not make David's tragic mistake.

—*Facing Your Giants*

Adoptive parents understand God's passion to adopt us. They know what it means to feel an empty space inside. They know what it means to hunt, to set out on a mission, and to take responsibility for a child with a spotted past and a dubious future. If anybody understands God's ardor for his children, it's someone who has rescued an orphan from despair, for that is what God has done for us.

—*The Great House of God*

God's Spirit is like a father who walks hand in hand with his little child. The child knows he belongs to his daddy, his small hand happily lost in the large one. He feels no uncertainty about his papa's love. But suddenly the father, moved by some impulse, swings his boy up into the air and into his arms and says, "I love you, Son." He puts a big kiss on the bubbly cheek, lowers the boy to the ground, and the two go on walking together.

Has the relationship between the two changed? On one level, no. The father is no more the father than he was before the expression of love. But on a deeper level, yes. The dad drenched, showered, and saturated the boy in love. God's Spirit does the same with us.

—*Come Thirsty*

# "IT'S ALL RIGHT"

M ax, your dad's awake." I had been watching a movie on television. One of those thrillers that takes you from the here and now and transports you to the somewhere and sometime. My mother's statement seemed to come from another world. The real world.

I turned toward my father. He was looking at me.

His head was all he could turn. Lou Gehrig's disease had leeched his movement, taking from him everything but his faith . . . and his eyes.

It was his eyes that called me to walk over to his bedside. I had been home for almost two weeks, on special leave from Brazil, due to his worsening condition. He had slept most of the last few days, awakening only when my mother would bathe him or clean his sheets.

Next to his bed was a respirator—a metronome of mortality that pushed air into his lungs through a hole in his throat. The bones in his hand protruded like spokes in an umbrella. His fingers, once firm and strong, were curled and lifeless. I sat on the edge of his bed and ran my hands over his barreled rib cage. I put my hand on his forehead. It was hot . . . hot and damp. I stroked his hair.

"What is it, Dad?"

*He wanted to say something. His eyes yearned. His eyes refused to release me.*

If I looked away for a moment, they followed me and were still looking when I looked back.

"What is it?"

I'd seen that expression before. I was seven years old, eight at the most. Standing on the edge of a diving board for the first time, wondering if I would survive the plunge. The board dipped under my seventy pounds. I looked behind me at the kids who were pestering me to hurry up and jump. I wondered what they would do if I asked them to move over so I could get down. Tar and feather me, I supposed.

So caught between ridicule and a jump into certain death, I did the only thing I knew to do—I shivered.

Then I heard him, "It's all right, son. Come on in." I looked down. My father had dived in. He was treading water awaiting my jump. Even as I write, I can see his expression—tanned face, wet hair, broad smile, and bright eyes. His eyes were assuring and earnest. Had he not said a word, they would have conveyed the message. But he did speak. "Jump. It's all right."

So I jumped.

Twenty-three years later the tan was gone, the hair thin, and the face drawn. But the eyes hadn't changed. They were bold. And their message hadn't changed. I knew what he was saying. Somehow he knew I was afraid. Somehow he perceived I was shivering as I looked into the deep. And somehow, he, the dying, had the strength to comfort me, the living.

I placed my cheek in the hollow of his. My tears dripped on his hot face. I said softly what his throat wanted to, but couldn't. "It's all right," I whispered. "It's going to be all right."

When I raised my head, his eyes were closed. I would never see them open again.

He left me with a final look. One last statement of the eyes. One farewell message from the captain before the boat would turn out to sea. One concluding assurance from a father to a son, "It's all right."

—*Six Hours One Friday*

It's much
easier to die
like Jesus if
you have lived
like him for
a lifetime.

—*No Wonder They
Call Him the Savior*

# WHAT MATTERS MOST?

Some years ago I witnessed a father taking prayer seriously during a Sunday morning worship service. As we took communion, I heard a small boy asking, "What's that, Daddy?" The father explained the meaning of the bread and then offered a prayer. The boy was quiet until the cup was passed. Again he asked, "What's that, Daddy?" The father began again, explaining the blood and the cross and how the wine symbolizes Jesus' death. Then he prayed.

I chuckled at the colossal task the father was tackling. When I turned to give him a knowing nod, I realized the father was David Robinson, NBA basketball player for the San Antonio Spurs. Sitting on his lap was his six-year-old son, David Jr.

Less than twenty-four hours earlier David had led the Spurs in scoring in a play-off game against the Phoenix Suns. Within twenty-four hours David would be back in

Phoenix, doing the same. But sandwiched between the two nationally televised, high-stakes contests was David the dad. Not David the MVP or Olympic Gold Medal winner, but David the father, explaining holy communion to David the son.

Of the events of that weekend, which mattered most? The basketball games or the communion service? Which will have eternal consequences? The points scored on the court? Or the message shared at a church? What will make the biggest difference in young David's life? Watching his dad play basketball or hearing him whisper a prayer?

—*Fearless*

I f your children have a faith like yours, what kind of faith will they have?

Parents, what are your children learning from your worship? Do they see the same excitement as when you go to a basketball game? Do they see you prepare for worship as you do for a vacation? Do they see you hungry to arrive, seeking the face of the Father? Or do they see you content to leave the way you came?

They are watching. Believe me. They are watching.

Do you come to church with a worship-hungry heart? Our Savior did.

May I urge you to be just like Jesus? Prepare your heart for worship. Let God change your face through worship. Demonstrate the power of worship.

—*Just Like Jesus*

"If you, then, though you are evil, know how to give good gifts to your children, how much more will your Father in heaven give good gifts to those who ask him!"

*Matthew 7:11*

# A FATHER'S DAY
# REMEMBRANCE

Today is Father's Day. A day of cologne. A day of hugs, new neckties, long-distance telephone calls, and Hallmark cards.

I remember my first Father's Day without a father. Perhaps you do too.

For thirty-one years I had a father. I had one of the best. But now he's gone. He's buried under an oak tree in a west Texas cemetery. Even though he's gone, his presence is very near—especially today.

It seems strange that he isn't here. I guess that's because he was never gone. He was always close by. Always available. Always present. His words were nothing novel. His achievements, though admirable, were nothing extraordinary.

But his presence was.

Like a warm fireplace in a large house, he was a source of comfort. Like a sturdy porch swing or a big-branched elm in the backyard, he could always be found . . . and leaned upon.

During the turbulent years of my adolescence, Dad was one part of my life that was predictable. Girlfriends came and girlfriends went, but Dad was there.

Football season turned into baseball season and turned into football season again and Dad was always there. Summer vacation, homecoming dates, algebra, first car, driveway basketball—they all had one thing in common: his presence.

And because he was there life went smoothly. The car always ran, the bills got paid, and the lawn stayed mowed. Because he was there the laughter was fresh and the future was secure. Because he was there my growing up was what God intended growing up to be: a storybook scamper through the magic and mystery of the world.

Because he was there we kids never worried about things like income tax, savings accounts, monthly bills, or mortgages. Those were the things on Daddy's desk.

We have lots of family pictures without him. Not because he wasn't there, but because he was always behind the camera.

He made the decisions, broke up the fights, chuckled

at Archie Bunker, read the paper every evening, and fixed breakfast on Sundays.

*He didn't do anything unusual. He only did what dads are supposed to do—be there.*

He taught me how to shave and how to pray. He helped me memorize verses for Sunday school and taught me that wrong should be punished and that rightness has its own reward. He modeled the importance of getting up early and staying out of debt. His life expressed the elusive balance between ambition and self-acceptance.

He comes to mind often. When I smell "Old Spice" aftershave, I think of him. When I see a bass boat I see his face. And occasionally, not too often, but occasionally when I hear a good joke (the kind Red Skelton would tell), I hear him chuckle. He had a copyright chuckle that always came with a wide grin and arched eyebrows.

Daddy never said a word to me about sex or told me his life story. But I knew that if I ever wanted to know, he would tell me. All I had to do was ask. And I knew if I ever needed him, he'd be there.

Like a warm fireplace.

Maybe that's why my first Father's Day without him was a bit chilly. The fire had gone out. The winds of age swallowed the late splendid flame, leaving only golden embers. But there was a strange thing about those embers . . . stir them a bit and a flame will dance. It will dance only briefly, but it will dance. And it will knock just enough chill out of the air to remind me that he is still—in a special way, even today—very present.

—*God Came Near*

God has
proven himself
as a faithful
father. Now
it falls to us
to be trusting
children.

*—He Still Moves Stones*

# SHOW UP

As God blessed my ministry, more and more calls came in from all over the world, wanting me to speak at churches, conferences, and grand openings of supermarkets. It was hard to say no at first. I felt every opportunity was from God.

Finally I realized that every time I said yes to something, I had to say no to something else. It's called Max's Yes Law of Inverse Dynamics. *Look it up!* It says this: with every yes in your schedule, there is an equal and opposite no reaction.

When I said yes to another speaking engagement, I said no to another family dinner.

When I said yes to another meeting, I said no to my girls' volleyball game.

When I said yes to another book tour, I said no to taking a walk with my wife.

So how do we show people that we love and believe in them? There are many ways to express those feelings— verbal affirmations, love letters, phone calls, even a quick text message saying, "I'm thinking of you." They're all good, but there's one that's the best.

I talked about it in my book *A Love Worth Giving*:

> Do you believe in your kids? Then show up. Show up at their games. Show up at their plays. Show up at their recitals. It may not be possible to make each one, but it's sure worth the effort . . . You want to bring out the best in someone? Then show up.

Now that my girls are all grown up, believe me, I'm glad I made that decision to show up before it was too late. Now (cue "Cat's in the Cradle" in the background) I miss those Meet the Teacher Nights and seeing their papier-mâché volcano at the science fair and sitting in the stands at the big volleyball meet, even if they were on the bench the whole time.

When it comes to kids and family, it is a lot easier to make money than to make up lost time.

—*Max on Life*

As God revealed himself to his children . . . they saw him as more than a mighty force. They saw him as a loving Father who met them at every crossroad of their lives.

—The Great House of God

# RELYING ON A
# DAD'S STRENGTH

Team Hoyt consists of a father-son squad: Dick and Rick. They race. They race a lot. Sixty-four marathons. Two hundred and six triathlons. Six triathlons at Ironman distance. Two hundred and four 10K runs. Since 1975, they've crossed nearly a thousand finish lines. They've even crossed the USA. It took them forty-five days to run and pedal 3,735 miles, but they did it.

Team Hoyt loves races. But only half of Team Hoyt can run. Dick, the dad, can. But Rick's legs don't work, nor does his speech. At his birth in 1962, the umbilical cord wrapped around his neck, starving oxygen from his brain, stealing coordination from his body. Doctors gave no hope for his development.

Dick and his wife, Judy, disagreed with the prognosis. Rick couldn't bathe, dress, or feed himself, but he could think. They knew he was bright. So they enrolled him in public school. He graduated. He entered college and gradu-ated again.

But Rick wanted to run. At age fifteen, he asked his dad if they could enter a five-mile benefit race. Dick was not a runner, but he was a father, so he loaded his son in a three-wheeled wheelchair, and off they went. They haven't stopped since.

Young Rick Hoyt relies on his dad to do it all: lift him, push him, pedal him, and tow him. Other than a willing heart, he makes no contribution to the effort. Rick depends entirely on the strength of his dad.[2]

God wants you to do the same.

*—3:16: The Numbers of Hope*

et God give you what your family doesn't. Let him fill the void others have left. Rely upon him for your affirmation and encouragement. Look at Paul's words: "You are God's child, and *God will give you the blessing he promised*, because you are his child" (Galatians 4:7 NCV).

—*He Still Moves Stones*

Our God is no fair-weather Father.
He's not into this love-'em-and-
leave-'em stuff. I can count on
him to be in my corner no matter
how I perform. You can too.

—*Max on Life*

Someday the children will understand why I was so busy."

But you know the truth, don't you? You know even before I write it. You could say it better than I.

*Some days never come.*

And the price of practicality is sometimes higher than extravagance.

But the rewards of risky love are always greater than its cost.

Go to the effort. Invest the time. Write the letter. Make the apology. Take the trip. Purchase the gift. Do it. The seized opportunity renders joy. The neglected brings regret.

*—And the Angels Were Silent*

# CLUTCHING OUR
# TOYS TIGHTLY

Years ago, I took my two oldest daughters to Sea
World. My wife was out of town, so Jenna, Andrea,
and I went to spend the day watching the dolphins dip,
the walruses waddle, and the penguins paddle.

We had a great day. Hot dogs. Ice cream. Stuffed
whales. Toys, toys, and toys. The girls know their dad is
a pushover for a thirteen-letter "Pleeeeeeeeese." I should
have known better. The average interest in amusement
park memorabilia is twelve minutes and thirty-two seconds. Then it is, "Daddy, can you hold this? It's too heavy."

"Now, I told you not to buy it if you couldn't hold
on to it."

"Pleeeeeeeese."

So, by the end of the day I was carrying two pen-
and-pencil sets, one set of sunglasses, an inflated
penguin, a shark's tooth (complete with shark), a life-
sized stuffed version of Shamu the killer whale, six
balloons, and a live turtle. (OK, I'm exaggerating; there

were only five balloons.) Add to that the heat, the rash from getting splashed with salt water, and the Eskimo Pie that melted down my shirt, and I was ready for a break.

That's why I was glad to see the plastic ball pit. This one activity is enough to convince you to keep your season pass current. It's a large, covered, shady, cool, soothing pavilion. Under the awning is a four-foot-deep pit the size of a backyard pool. But rather than being filled with water, it is loaded with balls—thousands and thousands of plastic, colorful, lightweight balls.

In the center of the pit is a sort of table with holes through which blow jets of air. Kids climb though the pit, grab balls, place them over the holes, and "Whee!"— up fly the balls.

The greatest part of the pit is the parents' area. While the kids roll and romp in the balls, the parents sit on the carpeted floor next to the pit and rest.

My oldest daughter, Jenna, did great. She dove in and made a beeline to the table.

Three-year-old Andrea, however, had a few difficulties. As soon as she took one step into the pit, she filled her arms with balls.

Now, it is hard enough to walk through the waist-high pit of balls with your arms spread to keep your balance. It is *impossible* to do it with your arms full.

Andrea took a step and fell. She tried to wrestle her way up without releasing the balls. She couldn't. She began to cry. I walked over to the edge of the pit.

"Andrea," I said gently, "let go of the balls, and you can walk."

"No!" she screamed, wiggling and submerging herself beneath the balls. I reached in and pulled her up. She was still clutching her armful of treasures.

"Andrea," her wise, patient father said, "if you'll let the balls go, you'll be able to walk. Besides, there are plenty of balls near the table."

"No!"

She took two steps and fell again.

Parents aren't supposed to go into the pit. I tried to reach her from the edge, but I couldn't. She was somewhere under the balls, so I spoke toward the area where she had fallen. "Andrea, let go of the balls so you can get up."

I saw a movement under the balls. "Nooo!!"

"Andrea," spoke her slightly agitated father. "You could get up if you would let go of . . ."

"Nooooo!!!!!"

"Jenna, come here and help your sister up."

By now the other parents were beginning to look at me. Jenna waded through the balls toward her little sister. She reached down into the pit and tried to help Andrea onto her feet. Jenna wasn't strong enough, and Andrea couldn't help because she was still clutching the same balls she had grabbed when she first stepped into the pit.

Jenna straightened up and shook her head at me. "I can't get her up, Daddy."

"Andrea," her increasingly irritated father said loudly, "let go of the balls so you can get up!"

The cry from beneath the balls was muffled, but distinct. "Nooooo!!!!!"

"Great," I thought to myself. "She's got what she wants, and she's going to hold on to it if it kills her."

"Jenna," her visibly angered father said sternly. "Take those balls away from your sister."

Down Jenna dove, digging through the balls like a puppy digging through the dirt.

*I knew she had found her little sister
and that the two were engaged in mortal
combat when waves of balls began
to move on the surface of the pit.*

By now the other parents were whispering and pointing. I looked forlornly at the employee who was monitoring the pit. I didn't even have to say a word. "Go on in," he told me.

I waded through the balls to my two angels, broke the death-locks they had on each other, put one under each arm, and carried them to the center of the pit. I dropped them next to the table (all the other kids scrambled away when they saw me coming). Then I marched back to the side of the pit and sat down.

As I watched the girls play with the balls, I asked myself, "What is it that makes children immobilize themselves by clutching toys so tightly?"

I winced as a response surfaced. "Whatever it is, they learned it from their parents."

Andrea's determination to hold those balls is nothing compared to the vice-grips we put on life. If you think Jenna's job of taking the balls away from Andrea was tough, try prying our fingers away from our earthly treasures. Try taking a retirement account away from a fifty-five-year-old. Or try convincing a yuppie to give up her BMW. Or test your luck on a clotheshorse and his or her wardrobe. The way we clutch our possessions and pennies, you'd think we couldn't live without them.

Ouch.

—*The Applause of Heaven*

The earnest prayer of a righteous person has great power and produces wonderful results.

*James 5:16* NLT

# SEEING OUR
# FATHER EYE TO EYE

Several years after Dad's death I received a letter from a woman who remembered him. Ginger was only six years old when her Sunday school class made get-well cards for ailing church members. She created a bright purple card out of construction paper and carefully lined it with stickers. On the inside she wrote, "I love you, but most of all God loves you." Her mom baked a pie, and the two made the delivery.

Dad was bedfast. The end was near. His jaw tended to drop, leaving his mouth open. He could extend his hand, but it was bent to a claw from the disease.

Somehow Ginger had a moment alone with him and asked a question as only a six-year-old can: "Are you going to die?"

He touched her hand and told her to come near. "Yes, I am going to die. When? I don't know."

She asked if he was afraid to go away. "Away is heaven," he told her. "I will be with my Father. I am ready to see him eye to eye."

About this point in the visit, her mother and mine returned. Ginger recalls:

> My mother consoled your parents with a fake smile on her face. But I smiled a big, beautiful, *real* smile, and he did the same and winked at me.
>
> My purpose for telling you all this is my family and I are going to Kenya. We are going to take Jesus to a tribe on the coast. I am very scared for my children, because I know there will be hardships and disease. But for me, I am not afraid, because the worst thing that could happen is getting to see "my Father eye to eye."
>
> It was your father who taught me that earth is only a passing through and death is merely a rebirth.

A man near death winking at the thought of it. Stripped of everything? It only appeared that way. In the end Dad still had what no one could take. And in the end that is all he needed.

—*You'll Get Through This*

God is the father pacing the porch. His eyes are wide with his quest. His heart is heavy. He seeks his prodigal. He searches the horizon. He examines the skyline, yearning for the familiar figure, the recognizable gait. His concern is not the business, his investments, his ownings. His concern is the son who wears his name, the child who bears his image. You.

He wants you home.

—*And the Angels Were Silent*

# STUCK BY A SHORTCUT

The Fourth of July. Everything about the holiday was red, white, and blue. My face was red, the clouds were cotton white, and the sky was a brilliant blue. My redness came not from sunburn but humiliation. Denalyn had warned, "Remember, Max, the lake level is low." The depth finder had alerted: thirty feet, then ten, then five, and then three feet. The caution buoys bobbed up and down in the water. But did I listen to Denalyn? Pay attention to the depth radar? Take note of the shallow-water markers?

Who had time for such trivialities? My three teenage daughters and their friends were counting on my navigational skills for a Saturday of entertainment. I would not disappoint. Wearing sunglasses and a big-brimmed hat, I hammered the throttle, and off we went. *Zoom!* Then five minutes later, boom! I had driven the boat onto a sandbar.

Passengers lurched forward. I nearly fell out. Seven sets of eyes glared at me. A lesser man might have told everyone to get out and push the boat back into deep water. Not me. Not throttle-happy Max. No sir. I was captain of the outboard, sovereign of the lake. I would debank the boat the manly way. I shoved the throttle again.

The boat didn't budge.

"Max," Denalyn kindly opined, "you messed up." I raised the rudder. It was bent like a dog's ear. This time we had no choice. We pushed until we floated. When I started the engine, the boat vibrated like a three-wheeled jalopy. Our speed peaked out at five miles per hour. As we chug-chugged across the lake and the other vacationers stared and the teenagers sulked, I asked myself, *Well, Captain Max, what were you thinking?*

That was the problem. I *wasn't* thinking. Dumb became dumber because I treated a bad decision with a poor, impulsive choice. Forgivable in a boat. But in life? . . .

Turbulent times will tempt you to forget God. Shortcuts will lure you. Sirens will call you. But don't be foolish or naive. Do what pleases God. Nothing more, nothing less. And for heaven's sake, think twice before you press that throttle.

—*You'll Get Through This*

In him lie hidden all the treasures
of wisdom and knowledge.

*Colossians 2:3* NLT

# DIRECTIONS FROM
# A DAUGHTER

On a trip to the United Kingdom, our family visited a castle. In the center of the garden sat a maze. Row after row of shoulder-high hedges, leading to one dead end after another. Successfully navigate the labyrinth, and discover the door to a tall tower in the center of the garden. Were you to look at our family pictures of the trip, you'd see four of our five family members standing on the top of the tower. Hmmm, someone is still on the ground. Guess who? I was stuck in the foliage. I just couldn't figure out which way to go.

Ah, but then I heard a voice from above. "Hey, Dad." I looked up to see Sara, peering through the turret at the top. "You're going the wrong way," she explained. "Back up and turn right."

Do you think I trusted her? I didn't have to. I could have trusted my own instincts, consulted other confused tourists, sat and pouted and wondered why God would let this happen to me. But do you know what I did? I listened. Her vantage point was better than mine. She was above the maze. She could see what I couldn't.

Don't you think we should do the same with God? "God is . . . higher than the heavens" (Job 22:12 TLB). "The LORD is high above all nations" (Psalm 113:4 NASB). Can he not see what eludes us? Doesn't he want to get us out and bring us home? Then we should do what Jesus did.

Rely on Scripture. Doubt your doubts before you doubt your beliefs. . . . God is constantly and aggressively communicating with the world through his Word. God is speaking still!

—*Next Door Savior*

Years ago a friend gave me this counsel: "Make a list of all the lives you would impact by your sexual immorality." I did. Every so often I reread it. "Denalyn. My three daughters. My son-in-law. My yet-to-be-born grandchildren. Every person who has ever read one of my books or heard one of my sermons. My publishing team. Our church staff." The list reminds me: one act of carnality is a poor exchange for a lifetime of lost legacy.

Dads, would you intentionally break the arm of your child? Of course not. Such an action would violate every fiber of your moral being. Yet if you engage in sexual activity outside of your marriage, you will bring much more pain into the life of your child than would a broken bone.

—*You'll Get Through This*

When my oldest daughter was in high school, she ran for office. She had a great slogan: "Vote for Jenna, she's a winna!" She lost by one vote. When I heard the news, I enlisted the help of some friends to create a large sign for our front yard. It ran across the width of the house. When Jenna pulled up in the driveway, she read these words: "Jenna, You're Still Our Winna!"

—Max

# COVERING A
# CHILD'S MISTAKE

The bank once sent me an overdraft notice on the checking account of one of my daughters. I encouraged my college-age girls to monitor their accounts. Even so, they sometimes overspent.

What should I have done? Let the bank absorb it? They wouldn't. Send her an angry letter? Admonition might have helped her later, but it wouldn't have satisfied the bank. Phone and tell her to make a deposit? Might as well tell a fish to fly. I knew her liquidity. Zero.

Transfer the money from my account to hers? Seemed to be the best option. After all, I had $25.37. I could replenish her account and pay the overdraft fee as well.

Besides, that was my job. Don't get any ideas. If you're overdrawn, don't call me. My daughter can do something you can't do: she can call me Dad. And since she calls me Dad I did what Dads do. I covered my daughter's mistake.

When I told her she was overdrawn, she said she was sorry. Still, she offered no deposit. She was broke. She had one option: "Dad, could you . . ." I interrupted her sentence. "Honey, I already have." I met her need before she knew she had one.

—*Cure for the Common Life*

By calling us home, God is doing what any father would do. He is providing a better place to rest.

—*A Gentle Thunder*

# BRING YOUR
# CHILDREN TO JESUS

"Pour out your heart like water before the face of the Lord. Lift your hands toward Him for the life of your young children" (Lamentations 2:19 NKJV).

Dads, we can do this. We can be loyal advocates, stubborn intercessors. We can take our parenting fears to Christ. In fact, if we don't, we'll take our fears out on our kids. Fear turns some parents into paranoid prison guards who monitor every minute, check the background of every friend. They stifle growth and communicate distrust. A family with no breathing room suffocates a child.

On the other hand, fear can also create permissive parents. For fear that their child will feel too confined or fenced in, they lower all boundaries. High on hugs and low on discipline. They don't realize that appropriate discipline is an expression of love. Permissive parents.

Paranoid parents. How can we avoid the extremes? We pray.

Prayer is the saucer into which parental fears are poured to cool. Jesus says so little about parenting, makes no comments about spanking, breast-feeding, sibling rivalry, or schooling. Yet his actions speak volumes about prayer. Each time a parent prays, Christ responds. His big message to moms and dads? Bring your children to me. Raise them in a greenhouse of prayer.

When you send them off for the day, do so with a blessing. When you tell them good night, cover them in prayer. Is your daughter stumped by geography homework? Pray with her about it. Is your son intimidated by the new girl? Pray with him about her. Pray that your children have a profound sense of place in this world and a heavenly place in the next.

—*Fearless*

# OUR COMING GROOM

Jesus elevates funerals to the same hope level as weddings. From his perspective the trip to the cemetery and the walk down the aisle warrant identical excitement.

This point struck home in our home when we were in the throes of planning a wedding. I use the word *we* loosely. Denalyn and our daughter Jenna planned the wedding. I smiled and nodded and signed the checks. Our house bustled with talk of bridal gowns, wedding cakes, invitations, and receptions. The date was set, church reserved, and excitement high. Weddings are great news!

So, says Jesus, are funerals. Both celebrate a new era, name, and home. In both the groom walks the bride away on his arm. Jesus is your coming groom. "I will come and get you . . ." He will meet you at the altar. Your final glimpse of life will trigger your final glimpse of him.

—*Fearless*

God has a
heart for
hurting parents.
Should we be
surprised? After
all, God himself
is a father.

—*Fearless*

# JESUS RESPONDS TO
# A DAD'S PRAYER

If you struggle with prayer, I've got just the guy for you. Don't worry, he's not a monastic saint. He's not a calloused-kneed apostle. Nor is he a prophet whose middle name is Meditation. He's not a too-holy-to-be-you reminder of how far you need to go in prayer. He's just the opposite. A fellow crop duster. A parent with a sick son in need of a miracle. The father's prayer isn't much, but the answer is and the result reminds us: the power is not in the prayer, it's in the one who hears it.

He prayed out of desperation. His son, his only son, was demon-possessed. Not only was he a deaf mute and an epileptic, he was also possessed by an evil spirit. Ever since the boy was young, the demon had thrown him into fires and water.

Imagine the pain of the father. Other dads could watch their children grow and mature; he could only watch his suffer. While others were teaching their sons an occupation, he was just trying to keep his son alive.

What a challenge! He couldn't leave his son alone for a minute. Who know when the next attack would come? The father had to remain on call, on alert twenty-four hours a day. He was desperate and tired, and his prayer reflects both.

"If you can do anything for him, please have pity on us and help us."

Listen to that prayer. Does it sound courageous? Confident? Strong? Hardly. . . .

He wasn't much of a pray-er. And his wasn't much of a prayer. He even admits it! "I do believe," he implored. "Help me to believe more" (see Mark 9:24).

This prayer isn't destined for a worship manual. No Psalm will result from his utterance. His was simple—no incantation or chant. But Jesus responded. He responded, not to the eloquence of the man, but to the pain of the man.

—*He Still Moves Stones*

If something is important to you, it's important to God.

Dads know that. Imagine if you noticed an infected sore on the hand of your five-year-old son. You ask him what's wrong, and he says that he has a splinter. You ask him when it happened. He says last week! You ask him why he didn't tell you, and he says, "I didn't want to bother you. I knew you had all those things to do running the household and all; I didn't want to get in your way."

"Get in my way? Get in my way! I'm your dad. You're my son. My job is to help. I hurt when you hurt."

—*He Still Moves Stones*

# A WORK IN PROGRESS

Everything worthwhile takes time to make. Wine. Sculptures. Paintings. Bridges.

However, we want the perfect kids to get perfect grades and pick the perfect college.

Sound perfect? Sure.

Sound probable? No.

Be patient. Your kids will not be perfect, at least not right away. Over time and with hard work, things fall into place. Maybe not perfect, but perfectly all right.

God is not finished with you yet. He's putting the final touches on your kids.

Be patient and don't give up before the Master nods approvingly, "Well done."

—*Max on Life*

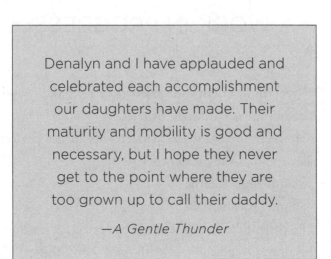

Denalyn and I have applauded and celebrated each accomplishment our daughters have made. Their maturity and mobility is good and necessary, but I hope they never get to the point where they are too grown up to call their daddy.

—*A Gentle Thunder*

Jesus did for us what I once did for one of my daughters in the shop at New York's La Guardia Airport. The sign above the ceramic pieces read Do Not Touch. But the wanting was stronger than the warning, and she touched. And it fell. By the time I looked up, ten-year-old Sara was holding the two pieces of the New York City skyline. Next to her was an unhappy store manager. Over them both was the written rule. Between them hung a nervous silence. So I did what dads do. I stepped in. "How much do *we* owe you?" I asked.

How was it that I owed anything? Simple. She was my daughter. And since she could not pay, I did.

—*Next Door Savior*

# OUR JOB IN THE
# MEANTIME—TRUST

It's a simple scenario. The Father has gone away for a while. But he will return. And until then, he wants his children to be at peace.

I want the same for my three daughters.

I left them once, when they were younger, so I could get away and finish a book. With a kiss and a hug, I walked out the door and promised to return. Did I want to leave them? No. But this book needed some work, and the publisher needed a manuscript, so there I was—in a hideaway—pounding a computer keyboard. We accepted the fact that a time of separation was necessary to finish the job.

While we were apart, did I want them to feel discomfort? Did I want them dreading my return? No.

What about denial? Would I have been pleased to hear that they removed my picture from the mantel and my plate from the table and were refusing to discuss my arrival? I don't think so.

How about disappointment? "Oh, I hope Daddy doesn't come before Friday night—I really want to go to that slumber party." Was I such a fuddy-dud that my coming would spoil the fun?

Well, perhaps I was. But God isn't. And, if he has his way with us, thoughts of his return won't disappoint his children. He, too, is away from his family. He, too, has promised to return. He isn't writing a book, but he is writing history. My young daughters didn't understand all the intricacies of my task; we don't understand all the details of his. But our job in the meantime? Trust. Soon the final chapter will be crafted and he'll appear at the door. But until then Jesus says: "Don't let your hearts be troubled. Trust in God, and trust in me."

—*When Christ Comes*

# NOTES

1. Jack Canfield and Mark Hansen, *Chicken Soup for the Soul* (Deerfield Beach, FL: Health Communications, 1993), 273.
2. David Tereshchuk, "Racing Towards Inclusion," Team Hoyt, https://franklyspeakingnow.com/Team_Hoyt.html.

# SOURCES

All of the material for this book was originally published in the following books or preached in sermons by Max Lucado. All copyrights to the original works are held by the author, Max Lucado.

*When Christ Comes*: Thomas Nelson,
*No Wonder They Call Him the Savior.* Nashville: Thomas Nelson, 1986.
*Six Hours One Friday.* Nashville: Thomas Nelson, 1989.
*The Applause of Heaven.* Nashville: Thomas Nelson, 1990.
*In the Eye of the Storm.* Nashville: Thomas Nelson, 1991.
*When God Whispers Your Name.* Nashville: Thomas Nelson, 1994.
*A Gentle Thunder.* Nashville, Thomas Nelson, 1995.
*The Great House of God.* Nashville: Thomas Nelson, 1997.
*In the Grip of Grace*: Thomas Nelson, 1999.
*He Chose the Nails.* Nashville, Thomas Nelson, 2000.
*A Love Worth Giving.* Nashville: Thomas Nelson, 2002.
*And the Angels Were Silent.* Nashville: Thomas Nelson, 2003.
*God Came Near.* Nashville: Thomas Nelson, 2003.
*Next Door Savior.* Nashville: Thomas Nelson, 2003.
*Come Thirsty.* Nashville: Thomas Nelson, 2004.
*It's Not about Me.* Nashville: Thomas Nelson, 2004.
*Cure for the Common Life*: Thomas Nelson, 2006.
*3:16: The Numbers of Hope.* Nashville: Thomas Nelson, 2007.
*Facing Your Giants*: Thomas Nelson, 2008.
*Just Like Jesus*: Thomas Nelson, 2008.
*Fearless.* Nashville: Thomas Nelson, 2009.
*He Still Moves Stones*: Thomas Nelson, 2009
*Max on Life.* Nashville: Thomas Nelson, 2010.
*Grace.* Nashville: Thomas Nelson, 2012.
*You'll Get Through This.* Nashville: Thomas Nelson, 2013.
Max entries were taken from sermons preached by Max at Oak Hills Church, San Antonio, Texas